LEVEE

Also by Paul Otremba

Pax Americana
The Currency

LEVEE

poems

PAUL OTREMBA

Four Way Books
Tribeca

This book is manufactured in the United States of America and printed on acid-free paper.

Four Way Books is a not-for-profit literary press. We are grateful for the assistance
we receive from individual donors, public arts agencies, and private foundations.

Library of Congress Cataloging-in-Publication Data

Names: Otremba, Paul, author.
Title: Levee : poems / Paul Otremba.
Description: New York, NY : Four Way Books, [2019]
Identifiers: LCCN 2019012395 | ISBN 9781945588419 (paperback : alk. paper)
Classification: LCC PS3615.T74 A6 2019 | DDC 811/.6--dc23
LC record available at https://lccn.loc.gov/2019012395

2nd printing, 2019

PROUD MEMBER

[clmp]

We are a proud member of the Community of Literary Magazines and Presses.

*For Holly, my whole family, and my friends,
for their love that reminds me every day
to find ways to love the world*

Contents

Floodplain Suite

Old Long Since   3
Climate Is Something Different   5
Between Dog and Wolf   7
Hail the Lizard   8
The Only Spider Named by Charles Darwin   10
Constellation   13
Like a Wide River   15
Suite America   17
Then on the Shore of the Wide World   21
Water Landing   23
Six Ways   25
Doctrine of That Bird Once Worshipped on the Shore   27

Course and Spiral

Course and Spiral   31

Levee

Good Morning, People   41
Midden   43
Twilight of the Gods   44
Cabin in the Woods   47
How Much Tremor There Will Be   49
The Abridged Politics of Starlings   51
The Representatives   53
Forty Million Daggers   55
Peripatetic   56
Red Telephone in a Secure Location   59
The Kremlin Mountaineer   60
Figure at the Base of a Crucifixion   62
The Palace   64

Morning Dew 66
The New Republic of California 69
Hard as It Seems 71
When They Looked Up, They Saw No One 73

Lock

Levee, Lock, & Dam 77
Aces/Eights 79
Sentences (Künstlerroman) 80
Badlands 84
Medical History 86
The Mountains of Madrid 88
The Dance 90
Gold Coast 92
The Extra Welcomes You to Sunnydale 94
Expectancy 95
Lives of the Saints 96
The Body Most Days 98
Portrait with Dust and Fingerprint 100
Cutman 102
After X 103
Vertigo 107
Nocturne with Emperor and Clown 110

Notes

Floodplain Suite

Old Long Since

It's a luxury to be this calm, this year
confettied over the wine-dark streets,

this city in its oil-fed night
sweats. We're going to need

a bigger rope and a long-game
scenario for our pyramid

schemes and makeshift shelters
offshore. So, you dig holes

for the cache of spent rods
now lighting up the floodplain;

I'll reconstruct the kissed and crushed
ends of the security services' cigarettes.

We were promised it would taste
like not tasting, just a chemical whiff

off of the still seeping horizon.
Remember to turn the camera on.

Remember to find a mule to bear back
the evidence engorging the balloon.

Add on *-ageddon* to convince them
we saw the chance, so we braced for it.

Climate Is Something Different

This was a heron, and the oddly effortless but dense wedge
its body made across the sky, and more odd for being unfamiliar,
landing on the puddled roof of the nearby frame shop,

the second day of the flood receding. Then, there was the crew
of red-vented bulbuls (which took me days of search terms
to identify—"black-crested bird with red breast," "bird with red chest,"

"bird red stomach," "bird" and "red" and "Houston"—when they invaded
last summer's ripened fig tree), the black-crested birds that came stowed
full of potential—mutated germs in the seedpods' husks—in cargo holds

of boats docked in the ship channel, before leaching into the city
like benzene jumping pipes for the Gulf. I mean this flood now abated,
yet still as it will be fifty, a hundred years from now, and you, gathered

on what shore you may have found there, you in this echo
I might have detected in pulses under the water's depth,
and—measuring them—have found myself also, does it help

I only wanted so I could have the need? What I denied myself had a border
as elastic as risen dough, the kind that requires a little heat and time
and teams of hungry organisms drunk and belching their conversions.

You are the life in you, like we here are the life in us. I tried spending
the better part of an hour last week casually dredging the net
for a record of the moment the microbiome takes up residence

with our bodies. To complain about the flood as only this flood
and then rue today's temperature is only sticking my hand outside
to get an estimate on the weather. I can report it is uncomfortable,

the air hovering on the edges of volcanic breath. If there is a lesson
on how not to worry, it's that you're not stuck only being one thing,
the multitudes in me and the multitudes in you. When ice-melt

exposes the bottle brought aboard the ship suspended on its journey,
whoever finds it might carry gratefully across their lips
these agents of the loop now circling through us.

Between Dog and Wolf

When I say quiet, I mean concentration,
each noise in chorus also its own voice: jay's call,
palm leaves and live oaks talking behind my back,
while an engine announces a stop sign's catch
and release. When I say calm and at ease,
I mean the scale is just wrong; the mite
remains in the bird's wing, the heat up for days,
which brought peaches a month early to this city
that will be shoreline long after anyone
can still reach here. It's not that it will happen
soon, but not soon enough to feel it
as satisfaction. Two nights ago I tracked
what I understood to be a hawk in its quiet
over houses until its infrequent wing beats
became lost in the backdrop of light
and the sky-colored glass of downtown.
It was the hour of the dog on the leash.
I watched until one master, then another was consumed
around a corner, before I went back inside to the news.

Hail the Lizard

The green anole lizard might
                    turn this way off
            its perch on the foxtail fern

into the circle of resting cats
                    or this way cutting a clear path
            to the cat's-claw vines invading

every seam in the fence.
                    At some point you just admit
            you're what remains of the tick

pinched free from the dog's flank
                    for constantly bringing to attention
            that the poet meant

perspective not resolve,
                    as in the anole's choice
            between two dark routes lying

equally in barb-cloaking leaves.
                    The poetry of the anole is not
            pedagogy. You are the sum total

of the anole leaping through
                 the lion's den of only half-sleepers
          who chase it up the fig tree.

You are the flash of the anole
                 toward the millipede, lost traveler
          on the concrete slab, and you are

the rival locked in the anole's jaw,
                 your triumph warming under
          a full sun. You are the dewlap's red

sun of warning, pulsing
                 from the trees. To fall down
          the face of the world, so effortlessly,

to venture out onto the thinnest
                 tongue of leaf, to be the hunger
          that hides in plain sight, false

chameleon, to be the anole
                 out of the cats' reach and the one
          whipping in the blue jay's beak.

The Only Spider Named by Charles Darwin

Dear portion, feared share, distributor of loot,
it's not just destiny but proof, ascertainment
of some natural law, neutral lot, I'd like to see

in your one face vibrating so swiftly you appear split
into three—spinner, lengthener, and the hard-bitten
hands twisting our ends into inventive shapes:

woman tosses live alligator to ex
across drive-thru window; rescuer's car rushes
to be sucked into flood's rapid surge;

lost couple found in frozen embrace
in thawed-out forest. No one is afraid
of what they should be, complained Horace.

It's simply enough to pass beneath
a branch of the storm-weakened live oak
or to move through this place in a body

playing telephone with its own cells,
a tumor like a dead zone dropping calls
in my stomach. How entering onto the patio's field

I feel the thread secured that says, "Where you go,
there I follow." Brushing it from my face,
I have the choice to think of it as air

around me amplified, every control
set on my skin cranked up to one just past
the decibel I hope—this time—won't harm me,

or to hedge for the odds, believing that
in each web cast, a bite lies hidden. Maybe it started
being raised in a crowded home where we needed

to wake early to hoard our small cut
of the daily allotment, but I find myself these days
scuttling around, accompanied by a private soundtrack,

some voice warbling cracked pieces of the dome
we live our lives staring up at, urging us to
Get it while you can. I've asked love into the room

only to have it watch me excuse myself into the hallway.
There've been spiders I've let live in corners
of the house and others I've dispatched swiftly

in the garden, knowing that even to slide back
the patio's glass door is to gamble
on a little sorrow. Spined fate,

the one upon whose back rides the mask
of a demon, fat as a grape, I learned too late
you were harmless. And you, the one delicately spun

from flakes of jade and light, if there existed
a reason that convinced me it was enough to know
the center where you waited, I couldn't explain.

Constellation

It's the space between them we can count on,
more constant than the light we claim
our fortunes by, and because we've proved
this janky wooden plank in the argument
we can proceed another premise, one body's-length
farther along the surface. You could bet
your hemlock on it or the next timid step
across the fogged-up mirror of the iced-over lake.
The state is ill; therefore, I am ill.
Hippocrates thought of the crab
because of its legs reaching out like tendrils,
like gossip's sideways whispering
through the crowd of swollen flesh.

Then, leaving my surgeon's office,
I had to step over the splayed fingers
of a spidering slick of oil in the parking lot,
which I tried to read like the lines in my palm.
My dreams, too, have become nebulous,
intense, and frequent, and just after waking
they take on the blankness of the bayou's face
when the stars black out behind clouds.
It's like a joke from some low-grade
and obvious comedy—how do you not get
out of the way of an oncoming steamroller?

I am learning the difference between urgency
and importance. Although, they often meet
at the more accusatory places. To the monarch
butterfly breaking loose of her chrysalis,
the twitter of the state is urgent.
The icy-blue eye of the flipped-over iceberg
has been here long enough to know what's important.
I place my hand against the window
and I'm met by the dark's aged coolness.
The light passing through me in many strands
from the cluster of bees set in the night sky
happened so fast and so many years ago,
there wasn't even a thought of me being born.

Like a Wide River

Raised along one, you understand things
                    about shores, how you come to believe in them, a glass
            blade slipped between here and there, letting fall clearly

that side and its woods, the shadows you walk into without leaving,
                    while here the street names like roots through leafmold
            make tributaries and trade routes across the map we call

mind; or there, it is woods to escape through, and beyond,
                    a marshland of roads to a city, a city you enter by exiting
            a shell left clinging to a reed along the bank, bending as the wind

bends it and moves you into a life sensed waiting, its wings veined
                    with currents already coursing through you. Here, if a shore,
            then somewhere to get to, a bridge suspended, that in another time

was a ferry to cross, the sun making spikes around a shade
                    that's your reflection, while unmoved hands work the oars.
            Or here, stretched out in the sun between two shallows

of unlit floor, the cat tips her eyes toward the light, two coins,
                    in this city built on bayous, those great shifters of runoff,
            fast food bags, plastic bottles, and an oily froth that feeds

the ship channel, then tossed upon the gates to the dead zone
        of the Gulf. You never see it, but 200,000 vessels and barges
    move 200 million tons of cargoed want and need

through the port each year, the promise of another shore,
        even as it's only an edge without definition,
    and even at its widest, the thinnest ink-stain of bird

or tree line lets you mark where the Mississippi ends,
        not in water forever falling off the lip, the world unable
    to exceed the squared-off pages of its atlas, even as it does.

Suite America

I walk these galleries where the light comes
from the walls, Mapplethorpe as a smiling Christ,
Mapplethorpe blossoming in furs, and here

he holds a switchblade, while his left hand plays
"Boy Bitten by a Lizard." In these rooms
we can only keep our smaller efforts

to stay strangers, our eyes meeting eyes tracing
movement caught in the curves of backs, mouths
open to receive mouths, and love's crowned dance.

Even the *nature morte*—a dirty sink
of the night's dishes spent, the Medusa's head
of expired tulips, the poppy's flared skirt

and the poppy's tip closed like a seed—hold
a vital charge I'm afraid was never ours.

***

Sometimes visiting the halls of old portraits,
maybe merchants at their ledgers and maps
sharply lit, poring over desks shored-up

with deeds to ships that account for everything
reachable, the fear comes that in all ways
that really matter, we've found our limits.

We've probed; the grainy outlook beaming back
gives up the same results, so much abandoned
dust and ice. In the article on my nightstand,

the climate scientist is having trouble
sleeping, so drinks water by quiet glassfuls
at windows backed with unreadable night.

This charged site of appetite and pain matters
until it won't. Breaking over the news,
one mother reads the hurried stream of texts

her son sent moments before the gunman
entered the bathroom her son hid inside;
then another mother is interviewed

in front of a hospital while we watch
the thought meet and exit her: "We are here
for such a short time." Saying this, a space

formed off-camera where she stared, where time
used to be, before it returned to the slight
shudder of the net it had always been.

***

I was twelve, or maybe thirteen, alone
in the driveway, sending a basketball
over and over through the rim until

I felt part of that arc, and I'd think up
puzzles while I practiced, like all the ways
we might get each other wrong if the horse

I saw in my neighbor's field wasn't the horse
grazing in other minds, or the darker field
of possibility: either we were here

to play out some disturbed god's game, who had—
like us—grown bored, or, being too powerful,
this life formed the terms of our long confinement,

***

because things couldn't be how they told me.
The leather circling through my hands held
a world I could work against, and my body's

lift before my legs reset their spring seemed
enough proof for the day, lasting out time
as long as the floodlights could gather me in.

It happened slowly, a decade's grip worn down
until I woke finding there was nothing
to discover. We've known again and again

the ones who enter crowded rooms and unmap
lives without mercy. But I need to listen—
there are those who showed up for love, and will,

despite the murders' certainties,
despite what we think we know about us.

Then on the Shore of the Wide World

The city was in great panic, neighbors
crushing under neighbors, making a wave
of worry cresting an undercurrent
of resolve, which seemed natural because
in my dream a river marked the landscape
otherwise indistinguishable with snow
and a few pines rising, so a valley
even the city's mayor was prepared
to walk away from, out to the boats waiting
at the docks. Her eyes pushed past mine, and I knew
the official position wasn't planned for—
      not evacuation but exodus.
I couldn't name what was coming but felt
the truth of it like smoke announcing first
the building you see is as good as ash.
When I woke, the room was a dark wave, then
another falling, not to drive me down
but a massive body to bear me out—
a condition I could see no end to.
There was nothing inside the wave; then a line
I'd read was suspended in it: "beneath
an atmosphere as unrelenting as rock."
I named the city Nineveh.

      ***

                                        But it
won't help to think of it as a city,
although that's one way now to get your mind
around it, eight lanes and a loop to link
the extremities, a tree-lined tollway
for the privileged to escape in a hurry,
which is what it feels like, some gathering
and panicked vector, an irritation
pressing on the half-thought until it pops,
and when we imagine it for ourselves—
ice-melt, the woken virus, some sublime
rock on its immovable course—there are still
mineshafts to hunker down in, the makeshift
oil drum flotillas. Best collect our seedlings
and geniuses. Better for us to splice
our stories into roaches who'll survive.

Water Landing

That in the event the way was blocked—smoke
in the bulkhead, a tumble in the aisle—
there would be a procedure, yet something

instinctive, the hive suddenly organized
as a hive to make good with our escape.

That in the event, a map will appear
in your seat pocket, the nearest path clearly lit.

That in the event, the unexpected one
speaks up for the crowd, "I can report we've learned
how to swim," before applause crashes forth

throughout the cabin. For this landing, look
at the thing immediately to the side
of your desire. For this landing, we are mice,

and our work is to churn in the bucket
for the holes they discovered in their pantry
the exact moment their guests were expected
for the dinner party. That in the event,

there were actually two events running
side by side, the same ticket scanners
posted at each entrance. For this landing,

we will believe it was only ever
one event, for which it stands, indivisible.

That in the event, you are permitted
to return, not to prayer, but to some image
of having just looked up at the sky, the sun
blinding out the parking lot before you drift

from the service. That in the event, time
will slow; you could count the brown flecks
like seeds or pollen dusting your neighbor's eyes.

That in the event, you'll be accounted for,
regardless of the seat assigned to you.

Six Ways

—after Kobayashi Issa

Underworld

Where her house now sits
investors will gain a plot
    where they'll build a house.

*

Things Unto Things

Budding street; the green
bins of Amazon boxes,
    plastics, cans. NO GLASS.

*

The Neighbors

In the cats' full bowl
of water, the possum's face.
    In the window, mine.

*

Polis

Sick with news all day.
Viral jokes light the pillow,
   shortening the night.

*

The Guests

The ships never asked
the bulbuls where they would go.
   My figs don't either.

*

With Fur, Not Feathers

From whoever fell
on the live oak, the lit globe
   of crepe myrtle springs.

Doctrine of That Bird Once Worshipped on the Shore

—Houston, August 31, 2017

A marsh bird coasts
over the traffic light
flashing red, and hovering
farther out, a helicopter
stalls, its own version
of hummingbird, its thin
feeding tube an invisible
line opening communication to
the whole watching world,
to the empire opposite
this city under water,
now slowly emergent (more
resilient opportunities, they'll say),
a new century perhaps
of not-wars, anti-epic, no
rush to make ground
buckle and subdued beneath
concrete, rebar, asphalt, glass.
Here at the mouth
of the ship channel,
we know the color
of that sky, and
what makes it. For

this is the feathered-hour
of going or returning,
when white wings appear
folded into bronze, gold,
the phoenix like commerce
tethered to its laws.

Course and Spiral

Course and Spiral

—after Marina Zurkow's "Outside the Work: A Tasting of Hydrocarbons and Geological Time"

This is your water. There is no other water like it. This is where you sit.

You've been invited to this table to think about time, to make a meal of time.

To move through time like falling backward through tarmac, you bring the bottle to your lips and draw.

To get at the heart of it, open the valve; to get at the core of it, burrow and extract. You might think—as you would a glacier—time's mantle and liquid center, or the whorled shell, time's mollusk; but you see now it is in you, a toast to you.

You hear that purity has a temperature (-20° Celsius), and you can watch it be refined like a rabbit from a hat, but when you pass the water through your lips, both of you are changed.

Your feet are on this shore, sunk in the muck of it; and if a shore, then another side and somebody waving there. The taste of that.

The brightness and brine of bottarga.

So cynical, mullet, not even hatched and already the tired look of a mummy.

O, bottarga, "my mother's the sea… my father's the earth… my name is… my father's the sea… my mother's the earth… is my life…."

When were you not making a meal of time?

"I was plodding and plodding, just plodding along." Salt of the earth and all that.

You must get your hands in it, break the sardine bones fried in oil. And the eye looks back from its pit, its well, its bevel; it's supposed to.

The hand snaps off a fin like knowledge.

Did you know the mullet is the fish with the gizzard?

Packed in salt, roasted through, the mullet is the fish with the bird-like flesh you can pick apart with your fingers, siphon the feathers along your tongue.

No president calls to give this bird-fish reprieve.

Here's the story of the man and his fish. The ones that he catches and the ones he releases.

Notes for a parable: There was a man on the Gulf and his boat and the factory that desired workers who made the boat and time's devourers who desired time that desired a meal that desired workers who made the meal that made the fish desired, which in turn desired a man who desired a boat that only desired water because it had gasoline, which was only ever the desire of the bones to lie down.

The mullet's eye may yet be succulent; it desires more data.

The mullet's cheek is a sweet meat.

If mullet is served baked in a salt crust, there will be urges to yell, "Salt fight," and see what transgresses. But it never transgresses.

By now your plates are a small orbit around you. You can tell time with them like patterns of constellations.

That splatter of stars—there was the time of our first organisms, the ones that sank to the seabed of our centerpiece.

"Let's drink to the hardworking people." (And the hardworking people are the first to take up the song, but don't mistake it for the happiness of the hardworking people, the joy of work, the song of simple pleasure in the body's simple movement. This isn't that kind of story.)

Each time the verse comes around, somebody keeps refusing to "think," instead continues to "drink" to "the humble birth," which at first seems charming, then suspiciously careless, but what do you know? You're not even singing.

Every meal is a season, not just the set of signs within a season.

The story of the first mouth to accept the spoil on the tongue and to be consumed by the drinking of that beautiful transformation.

The song is old, as the story is old: "And such is the lot of everyone. I say, / therefore, brim the mixing bowls with wine, / for only in oblivion is oblivion braved."

There is a song in the heart and it goes: umeboshi butter, umeboshi butter, umeboshi butter.

By now your consumption is a congestion of satellites around you. And there lies the future that is the debris of the past and all its waves of pixels. The narrative, like the core, has shifted.

Sweet devourer, like a taste, a word brings back time to you.

There's a place in New Orleans called Coop's Place, where you'll find a decent bowl of gumbo, and you once met friends there.

Not just an aesthetic, the wit and whimsy of reordering the elements beneath your rigid expectations, but labor. You must work to make the experience, like someone works to make your experience. So, you assemble the disassembled dish.

Aspic domes of marine life dissolving in consommé. The anxiety of choosing your tutelary spirit that you'll let inside you as you eat. Or the anxiety of what your choice will tell on you.

Globes of roe like many radioactive eyes.

The narrative is important. The narrative is as old as dirt where you swirl the roux off the muddy spoon. Toil and trouble.

The *terroir* of farm-raised salmon is the grayness of clay. A SalmoFan™ can help with that.

"A natural antioxidant in the same family as the beta-carotene found in carrots," and so the prospect of finding what "fits the consumer's image of salmon flesh."

A rumor begins that there will be an event. Even a single meal has its micro-seasons.

In the distance, the plates wobble along their ellipse, come crashing into their star.

Out of the sea you'll emerge with time on your back to found a new habitat. An oyster slides along a tongue as it's done since prehistory.

A word brings you permission: the jellyfish locked in granita to unlock your hand now bringing the spoon to your lips.

You, dreamer, scooping up creatures like nostalgia for the future, whose color is the flesh of Texas grapefruit.

Someone once told you the landscape on the gulf of Texas is all in the sky, storms and vistas, suns going down like boiled crawfish shells, or a sky in the coolness of its blue looking glacial.

The story's old; don't poke among the pebbles.

But don't be fooled either. It was a river of oil that carried you here, leaking through sands, indiscreetly jumping deposits, and it oozes from you like sweat.

The time you've eaten bursts and gushes, eddies and pools.

And you leave its sludge, a print on a wineglass, as you force up a sweetness, the seepage rippling from your sphere.

Levee

Good Morning, People

Your mind is full of red,
declares Grace Slick to the morning
maniacs who resisted sleep all night
to catch the festival's second day close.

Yes, love would be better, even if it's the urge
to wait up for what's next
or, at least, the hope that someone
will be there for it. Who hasn't been treated

like a guest misstepping off the path
onto their host's newly planted
cornflowers? What I came here for
was the remembered video of Richie Havens,

what I experience as a need
to hear the lyric he's excavating through singing,
or like he's orchestrating the tangible evidence
of some infinitesimal star collapsed

in the air in front of him: "Sometimes I feel
like a motherless child." Who was it
40,000 years ago that in their boredom
or awe mixed a pool of spit with red ochre

and signed the cave wall with the outline
of their hand? Did they then retreat
to some further recess and think,
like an instinct, "What am I doing here?"

The deer grazed the stone idly; outside,
the wooly rhinoceros wouldn't stick around.
Sometimes when I see a horse in the fields
the county keeps as a median for the tollway,

I get the sad joy of being in the presence
of something unaccountably vast and old.
The grounds outside the prison in Huntsville
are full of horses, and there were days

driving past them when I found it unforgivable
to hang that image before the prisoners,
and moments I could imagine the profound calm
of that vision. "Freedom," Richie Havens draws

from the air around the stage, or it is a resource
deposited in the passages veined through him
that carries him to his feet, through onlookers
and crew, leaving the crowd with music offstage.

Midden

It could be worn stone, where water or wind
had visited, leaving behind scalloped bowls.
Perhaps the upturned curve of scapula
or cracked pelvis. Vast quantities of oysters,
a cheap and common food, were consumed
at the settlements. Could mean years.
Could mean hordes. The ice formed, then weakened.
He had gone past the point on the horizon,
then crossed back. It was a thin layer that year.
Roman tiles, an iron disk, fragments
of charred bone. She walked along the shore
collecting oyster shells, the hardened lips
of what had been loosened of their songs.
Which side meant sky? Which meant sea?
Perhaps it was a trade, a bargain not fully realized,
like the arrowhead accepted by the flesh.
Hands bound because the gods love talking
but not talking back. In the metaphor, the body
digs a cellar, stocks provisions for a siege
or hard winter. Then the waters opened
and took the ship whole. The waiter spoke
as you would to an accomplice—
what you're tasting is the sea.

Twilight of the Gods

It's what we mean when we say
the plot's edges meet
in the fullness of time,

but not cleanly, like the rough
approximation of a horse folded from paper
and left on the nightstand

the morning after, significantly, or here,
all the prisoners lined up in a row,
and across the linen shirt—

What an artist!—the promised stain
deepening. Or imagine
a timescale on earth

where all the ordinary hell we humans
have been raising in the story's untidy corners
can fit dancing on a sword tip

or sleep patiently in the fire.
Each new day is a day to commit
to forging things

that change other things, like putting on
a magic helmet. How I tossed the cat
faux-fur mice and avoided thinking

about his dragon's teeth.
How every ash tree in a field
has potential to be split.

But I'm grateful we have these chairs
to drag up the hill, with a space
designed specifically to hold our drinks,

while the performance moves toward its reward
in the amphitheater below.
It's the one where loyalty

means you're taken to a room offstage
and whipped. Where what bleeds
is both love and state.

Although life is more like a cycle,
interminable and propped up
by fanatics who would just as quickly

cut you in a brawl
as snub you at the gala.
You only need one clean hand

to wave thanks. You'll be fine
as long as your bow moves
in sync, and even then

the pit hides your mistakes.
Above, stars remain indeterminate.
Scarpia is dead;

his message sent.
The window sits open
to let Tosca take her breath.

Cabin in the Woods

We are at the point when the attic's antique lock
already is hacked open, when the trapdoor's dropped
on the preacher's hidden playroom, and clothes fall
across the seats of the borrowed convertible,
while the city is faraway but still awake

beneath the overlook, where no one's looking out
for what they should be, and the burial sleep
has been kicked up carelessly, because the dare
held the promise of touching, because a hint
of buttons strained to be undone, because it was raining

and there was nowhere to go besides this house—
empty—kept like a secret by kudzu off the road,
because the wealth of other lives is such a steal
at yard sales, who could say no to the music box,
the carved mask, the ancient and yellowing diary

with its small Latin script, a living hand—grasping
and capable—caught below the surface? For this night
(which is night because how else is this happening?)
you get to feel chosen. Like splintered pallets of wood
whose destinies are always to impale skulkers

of dark alleys, like the stripped bones and torn T-shirts
that mean torches for the dungeon's safe passage.
You even get a choice, your own devil shuffling cards
at the crossroads: this way, the table saw; here, the exit
wound; or Tunnel #3 for the breadcrumb-trail of blood

toward the final girl. There's no plot hole good violence
can't satisfy. In *these* worlds, with confidence, pull off
to change your tire after midnight inside the forest.
Pull in to this southern town where the motel is pure
vacancy. Trespass here is a foregone conclusion; prejudice,

incidental. So pound the stranger's door in your need.
The gauze of clouds across the moon will dim
your location among the houses. The stalks in the field
touch suddenly in chorus like so many wings. The emergency
axe hangs in the hallway waiting for someone's good idea.

How Much Tremor There Will Be

How quickly links move me through our country, first
thin reports, then the crowds redacted by smoke—
how slow the time for the boy left in the street.
I want to say it sears the mind, the burnt-out

canisters shown lying around their feet, shot
into people's lawns. (*Go home. I am home. You
go the fuck home.*) To do *that*, to stare into
submission while looking through the narrowing

scope—but not visible. How else to explain
that the eye rests there, holds fast the line cutting
against their refusal? *Bring it, you fucking
animals* caught on the hot mic. We see you.

We see you, the cameras would say, and still
they advance; one shouts a barrel in a face,
eye against eye and the fragile feel of it.
No eyes meeting real eyes, though, just the gauzy

film like cool milk poured into burning orbits,
like something smeared out of an infected root,
while the bewildered mouth's pressed into a plea—
"I can't breathe"—under the civic body's brute

enforcement. Justice? Look beneath your boot's tread,
but see, there's nothing to take back, nothing left
to exchange. That's the lesson's broken-glass edge,
that out from this lens appears simply a shape,

a description and you invoking it, where
he resists, charges, grabs at his waistband, and
you rest your cheek as in lining up the sights
or in going to sleep. He will never wake.

The Abridged Politics of Starlings

The cats made small effort at a meal
of the bird that had so anxiously looked
over the ground, and in the night something came

for the rest of it, an openness you can fit
everything into—right to the edges
of the yard, or the circumference

of your palm, the width of the shadows
pressed up against the light, long now,
but soon everything will be the flat disk

of afterlight—the cars, trees, and walkers,
leashes cutting angles with their dogs,
and the angels' arrangement, this street

and its government.
                    The committee has formed,
and at this hour you can get just close

enough before the swoop and shift
of resettlement on fences, branches,
in loud congress, the same show

each night, almost night—especially when
murmurs grow large in winter—
in what we call the hour of the eye

with its edges going jaundice. There is
a charter somewhere that accounts for
everything. How people sailed here

to trespass on the old ones, their ships
littered with a hundred songs and seed husks,
the shapes across the floor mirroring the sky.

The Representatives

When they showed up at my ready door,
it was their taste for flesh that misled me,
and it was a picture produced later
that confirmed what provisional and corrupt
intelligence we'll go on, and successfully.
They were not, as I previously reported, wearing
the same blue suit, so subtly pinstriped
it may have been only threads throwing
light as they shifted or leaves casting shade
as they moved in the wind, each suit accented
by the same tie or scarf, red and fat,
an open palm's width slapping where it dangled,
and they didn't share one face, a pale disc
accentuated by too-squared-off teeth,
a pudginess of indulgence improbably
occupying the same space as cheek bones
so sharp you could force a beer open off them.
I didn't recognize the nuances, the glances
scurrying behind their eyes staring out:
one was composed entirely of clawed
and crawling things, like langoustines
or crawfish, what the locals call mudbugs;
this one was colonized as if by larvae blooming
over cans of cat food someone so generously

left out for the strays. They had a foot thrust
in the doorway already when I politely tried
to explain I had no cash, no pen, no working
internet, but I'd consider the literature,
mail in the poll later. That's fine, one said tenderly.
Just fine, another's breath said hot at my ear.

Forty Million Daggers

They believe in their country pressed up against
the back of your mind, its hard circle, and cheer

the takedown, rough-riding bodies until they're just
bodies delivered, and their memories of a grand ole time

smack palms through the congregations, show up
as snail tracks on the crops or the fatted eye socket

reflected in the cruiser's warped hood, grated
by the waggled bulb's fracturing light. The current

to your neck provides unexpected results, the flips
and flops of having so many wars on. If not a word

first breathed across the waters, say, a lord of afterdays,
at least we might agree there was a little clay fed by deltas,

but all we can manage is the glass's weight sagging through
windows, fogged out, and a ghostly finger spelling *WORLD*.

Then feel out each day, act out each day, go to your loved ones,
say *I hear you*, each mouth a walled-in state bordering yours.

Peripatetic

—after Pablo Neruda and Tomás Q. Morín

I don't want to continue as a root and a tomb.
I don't want all this misery.
And I don't think I ever imagined a workable future,

or any future for that matter, reading in the bedroom
or basement or public park, although getting on
at Station A presupposed some notion of Station B.

And, of course, it's not like a train,
but more like a slide, if a slide were full of holes
falling onto other slides with still other holes

opening upon new surfaces to walk along,
this street onto this street, this block
of condos with 24-hour concierge, business

and fitness centers, or these homes hugging
lot lines. Each encouragement announced
for the continually updating optimal route

inevitably leading where? It's the kind of game
we can play interminably: Was it getting in the car
or not getting in the car? The absentee ballot

instead of just rolling over in bed?
If you ask me today, I'll say I'm tired,
while in front of the cameras, a man in all seriousness

claims if you inspect a gift horse's mouth
and discover rotten teeth, it's only the horse's
moral failing you are witness to. Of course,

it isn't about a horse, and the gift
is only a gift in the sense that you didn't ask for it
but woke to it in your bed sheets anyway.

I'd say prop him up, look him in the eyes,
if they weren't only divots plugged with coins
and palm ashes. His tongue is forked

and the tips can fill both his ears. What image
of the world does he summon forth
when his tongue beats the air?

You will live, but how? As a yes-man
in a too-fine-to-be-too-ill-fitting
costume, who escaped to Thessaly

only for the promise of an expensive meal.
Make Athens Great Again had never fit
onto the philosopher's ladder

of calculations. Of course, they tried
and did him in anyway. I was young
when I first read that, so was corruptible

and missed the point: if you introduce dialogue
in the first act, they still demand
a little death before it's over.

Red Telephone in a Secure Location

The meat part says "I" and "Please."
What tools the blade? It was video files,

drone-wrecks, precedented action for nighttime
raids. What full quench of protein

can I gather in my mind? It says the sky
cavities. It says keep the fingerprint

when completed. The puzzle answers
and her judgment should not seed

blame. See this homeland? Race? Cloud
of black-site councils with a ram's head

of stratagems? Of course it's in a name,
the tongue caked in florets of fine minerals,

his hands bound behind him so
as not in the way. I, who am registered

to savor many people, am moved by sounds.
Don't rush the questionnaire; take little feet.

The Kremlin Mountaineer

—after Osip Mandelstam's "The Stalin Epigram"

He moves through air like he's pressed to a lens.
He hears a crowd each time he holds a pen.

A child, he drew plans for a wall so huge
you could see it from space, then learned it was true.

For a week he woke from a single dream—a wolf
of the steppes—wet beneath his blanket' s wool.

He relieves himself. He lifts his belly's fold.
He knows which bolt is merely painted gold,

which pocket holds the real one. Every mirror
calls to him. Earbuds bloom in the off hours

around his offices, then hitch along
to the airstrip. The engines hide his songs.

When he thinks to express them, his hands swell
plumply like grapefruits. Most days they're navels,

puckered oranges playing in a plum's league.
Better a bird straining the eyes' fatigue

from glaring all night at a palmed, lit screen
than a convocation of eagles feeding

off scraps that leap from his mouth while reigning
over seas of love. If the room's constrained,

the marshal's in cahoots with the camera.
No one noticed through the rain's panorama

the drop caught in the deep crook of his eye,
when inside him a Bavarian sky

opened—he cried, "Papa!" His tongue waiting
like a leather strap to align the blade.

Asked for his favorite character in the tale,
he'd said Geppetto. He knew it was the whale.

Figure at the Base of a Crucifixion

—after Francis Bacon

In the middle of the phone call
    my whole body shook,
        something falling in me sending

a counterwave upward,
    what I felt unshrouding me—
        until I was only mouth—

into the air as if the air
    made a room, a cell with a chair
        or a table depetaling its legs,

a carpet like nails I could pluck
    to pierce the walls with—
        it wanted out,

which was the trespass
    because the choking off
        sound was me. So

Aeschylus has his Furies say:
        "The reek of human blood
                smiles out at me."

The Palace

It was some wished-for validation
Of the principle that a thing is not a thing
Until it's witnessed, so I wouldn't search
Until the reports came in, which did
(Poorly differentiated adenocarcinoma
With signet ring features), which meant
I finally looked up—numbers, graphs, expectancies
Abstracted. A car ride, in that moment, made sense.
Yes, groceries made sense. *But Paul, I hope*
You know that we're all here and we
Won't let your sleep upset you tonight.
The song from the car lingering with me
Down the aisles, the light touching every leafy thing,
Everything from ground or sea or field,
Each packaged thing out of field or sea
Or dirt or leaf, too bright, as if soaked through.
But Paul, there's something in your stomach
Turning sour. The song late to its own premonition.
So, I smiled to the man in the field-colored apron
Stocking energy water and to the woman
Whose shirt was a mountain lake I'd once seen
As my full cart passed her own full cart,
And I didn't look down from the young man

Facing me over the checkout counter. What happened
In my head still not true. *But Paul,*
We all must sleep, so go to sleep.

Morning Dew

All the quiet that carried me outside
        to ease my worried, my news-tangled mind
    and watch early lights sharpen the skyline,

which I've never found not there, not lit up,
        though I could think it, and have, once or twice:
    cratered glass and concrete, cracked stalks of steel

like bones come upon where some animal
        left them in the grass—and then the frayed sound
    through the speakers, the voice's break, "I can't

walk you out in the morning dew today."
        For years, I made the Grateful Dead's version
    a melancholy forecast of love's sad

requests and diversions. That is lost—fire
        stealing the horizon, or like a road
    my family once drove through South Dakota,

caught in a rainstorm's sudden and complete
        erasure, my arms rigid extensions
    of the wheel, while in the passenger seat

my father let the music continue
              consoling, it's nothing, merely a box
      of rain. Gone, but not as the song imagines.

I remember sitting at a crossroads
              where two Minnesota highways met, hearing
      over the radio that he was gone.

It was my first time to participate
              in the ritual: remember where you are
      when they die. Years later, visiting home,

my father handed me a slim column
              of newspaper, an obituary
      for another singer he'd saved for me

because he once heard me mention his name.
              What else to do but take it? Keep it safe
      in some drawer or misplaced box with the things

I told myself, "Save this, you'll need it."
              I should have seen my mistake when he sang,
      "Well, there's no need for you to be worrying about

all those people." Bonnie Dobson composed
           the song. 1961. Her good friends
       down on beds. California dropping to beds.

The dew in her vision was not a sign
           for anything other than real water,
       if water were radiant with a force

that could ignite the dust rising from sheets
           where her friends would no longer. I've also
       been terrified by dreams, waking ones too,

and avoided sleep, for a year in fact,
           afraid of what would come. Until one morning
       I'd forgotten what haunted me. Lately,

I've started waking again, the room dark,
           traces of the world's dream caught up with mine,
       and if I let myself go where my mind

would go, there's a sere and inhospitable
           landscape waiting for us to walk into,
       despite what we said mattered anyway.

The New Republic of California

I was not remembering the *Republic*—the cooked egg expertly peeled and split,
a more perfect union toppled by a hair—because that was love they split.

It's a problem with the math, being told to pick points on a map, then to imagine
your body in towns you'll never visit, the distance constantly split.

On this side, a landscape of prisons, pox, slumping extractions of minerals;
on that side, prayer groups and quarterly projections, so hardly a good split.

It's the recipe for taking what can't be lost and smashing it
from the charge and orbit, the spin of the matter/antimatter split.

The climate never lets you forget—water might get into the cracks
and freeze, so the face of the statue would split.

On this side, the hand-dipped rag full of gasoline; on that side, the same
hand offering the rag as a salve to your lip it had split.

I was ready to go Dutch, but your grand juries, emergency sessions,
and Sunday schools have racked up a bill I can't split.

So what if we cry, *Lightning*! *No hard feelings*! Then slap palms moving
through the line-up—*Good game. Good game*—just call the score a split?

Don't feel bad if you recognize you're just a little bit excited. Everybody knows when you come up aces, there's reward in just saying you'll split.

We still believe in fair warnings, like any good protagonist: *One if by late night host. Two if by C-SPAN.* Then I'll know to get back on my horse and split.

Hard as It Seems

It's become a thing I do, catching myself
catching myself and thinking, "How

unlikely?" The mind is its own dental office
waiting room. It started there for me, too, my never

taking well to the numbing. I've tried to hold
to the drill's mere being, the bright nerve

tweaked, the taste of something powdery
and singed falling down my throat. That pain

is yours, just as the sightline from the strip
of art deco apartments to the palm trees

anchoring the hills is for you. If I look farther
from this hotel window, that's the country

driving east, manifesting for us a spaciousness
of commentary on how we've gerrymandered

our options for this season. The enemy
of my enemy sits down for today's exclusive

surrogate interview. I draw the shades and say
to no one, "You get the news cycle you deserve."

All alerts point to everything continually breaking
with no plans to relent. Who would elect this?

The Committee for the Strategic Betterment
of the Conditions Inside the Volcano met

and their findings reassure us we're living
in the hardest working, most decent quarry

that ever existed. I'm in California
and I don't know where one would even go

to make a new start. The device on my wrist
tallies my steps from bed to desk, desk to bed,

and tells me I've almost reached my goal
of standing on the corner of Ocean and Elm.

When They Looked Up, They Saw No One

It would take a statue or a downsized god
to hold up such a thing. Step out of line

and you get to shoulder this sky.
With each silvered leaf cut from shadows

across the flats of sunrise is a small dome
puffy with agitation, like a hangnail's failed rebellion.

Justice just feels left out
from proportion. You can be reminded of that

every day. Picking two or three snails
from the damp shade beneath the nasturtiums,

then rolling them between rock and patio,
can appear sacrificial, especially when considering

the birds. Let's consider the birds.
This morning's dove who mistook its own reflection

was disturbingly limp when I lifted it into the nest
of plastic grocery bags—a profound accumulation—

I then buried in the trash, three sweltering days
before pickup. But yesterday, it was a palm's worth

collected from the sorrel, rosemary, and heather,
the shells shifting in my hand like a hefty sum

that would have been indecent to spend,
so I deposited them in the uncut grass

around the crepe myrtle, whose branches stretch
the scales between my neighbor's yard and mine.

Lock

Levee, Lock, & Dam

All this had happened before. So, I knew
that to open the basement door was to call up
disaster. Only, this time in the dream,
my brother and father were floating rafts
of belongings on the recurrent knee-deep water

that looked, each time I'd dreamed it, lashed
to the wheel of its final desire, wanting so much
to climb beyond itself, water meditating on water,
an unquiet thing, it would only expand
into that drowning. I tried to salvage

what I could into a tower of aging equipment:
VCR, tape deck, absurdly large speakers,
an ark for stories and songs I'd already lost
access to, as they sank below the sleep
I left behind. But the first time I woke last night

it was worse, and while I don't remember the dream
that broke me, if it had a color, it was empty concrete
pools slowly taking on rain, some growing sense
that in a future near enough, it will matter
to no one what shape it takes. A thought easy

to steer aside in the morning. Even as we'd slept,
the passages that rise or drop for hope
had continued their work. Someone's team
would be advancing. 70 people boarded a plane
and were taken down into the sea.

Aces/Eights

Why wouldn't I turn my back to you? Your fist
        called up so blood from my bent nose might run

as copper and salt in my mouth, whose look
        could have been the shit-eating grin of insight

if not knocked dumb that it could take a punch?
        Nights laid down flush and drunk over the waves,

pulled in rip currents of bad highs, bored trips,
        nights brought down over the mind to make room

for the loosener of limbs, shady gods
        begged from river, forest, gas-fed bonfire,

nights of clothes on the beach and police lights
        shot across my resources for going dark,

I tried spending you down like my body, weak stack
        of chips at your table, promise sprung from each hit.

Sentences (Künstlerroman)

Not red not a line but spots in a book and "L"
was for "Lion" so you get the idea

for your ideas somewhere.

Unremarkable really was the coterie of nails
for the tires of the rocks through the windows or the tag

now you're it—now show me

your room with the lights out.

A shed more like it for the spin and the kiss the smell
of gasoline and grass and look how strong how big

how the branch breaks.

And if the lovers get had what then I'll tell you
this dirty little fetch you a drink.

And what are they doing there a game there a circus
wheels around her laugh performed for him—

"Are they for *cereal?*"

So the couples all glint all bleached-out tooth thigh-gleam
uncrossing under the table that white dress short

conjures up the ice pick.

I didn't see first that flash that flesh

peek open it was a deck
of cards and his cock so big two hands

where he reached it.

That bird that cat box of rabbits hematoma like a brain
ballooning tufts of deer fur caught in the side panel

it wasn't the drugs that ruined Easter.

You want to come to hand she was kind
once her hands helped you finish.

It will hurt yes like swiveling an arm like a shoulder
popped that bone on the plate shows the mechanism.

Your brother's face he'd done it "I've ruined it"
you'd passed that mess by the roadside.

And when I've said it what then what liquor and a bicycle
in the rain after watching the actors' frenzied dance

on the screen then back inside to fuck there?

In the stories I read in my childhood basement how it happens
over centuries you get a spear through the chest through

the back through the face you get a bag for the cat
for the river where your love goes.

When the Lion returns the man who didn't know better
but was decent gets to walk outside see things

as they are yet wanders friendless—

I wanted to burn down the tent for his sake.

And if I say lion and you say lion and what I picture
is not what you picture so my moral thinking went.

I don't really miss it it was sad mostly it was petty
the hand always groping intimations of show me yours.

He said it was to knock out horses knock a hole where
your head went mush I never found much beyond

the hum though.

The premise was a sea captain picks her up overboard
all businesslike so the ride makes sense makes clothes

chart the floor I can watch she said for ten more minutes.

Does that do it for you you can say it we can tell
on us now all hands on ears on deck.

Badlands

Hunkered down and pocked, laid out like fingers
playing by terrible ear, and so much poverty

in the fossils' memories of flesh, those migrations
were interrupted long ago; they're told by the slow wave

of each scalloped pile's rusted striations. To be dry stone
in a season of mud; the "Oh Dear God, my leg!

My leg!" in the fall from the unwatched-for
height of it. Here, you glimpse the old infinities

scooped out before petering into plains. Satellites
prove it. And at that distance the rough surface makes

a permanent winter where typically you'd find
colorful veins. Filters can only make the light

vampire, rain-soaked, or Oregon Trail. Every morning
I resubscribe for the promise of the exclusive

cheat code. I've spent 30 lives going commando
from bed to coffee machine and back. Once, perhaps,

there was opportunity to make dramatic and right
decisions, the kinds arcades and the ever-rebooting

franchises were built for. The technology exists;
you can capture all my legs and arms off the ground

as I keep pace around the turn. The stables
of my best attempts are most attentive in early morning.

What image enters the horse's eye at that moment
of inexplicable pursuit through the open prairie?

It's what I imagine it feels like to charge down the hill,
but I'm only confronted by the plateau of the next rise

and the rise after that. It was a thought I had once
behind the window of a car my parents were driving

through South Dakota: for each solitary tower
of earth, I could place a single, solitary rider.

Medical History

Did you enjoy the sun so much
it hurt? The chemically refracted
sunsets the length of Houston's sky?

How often did you swim
in the runoff pool where bullheads
spawned and sumac grew an arsenal

for the neighborhood battles?
How much smoked meat?
Which grandfather's jacket

did you wear when sneaking outside,
snow deep around your calves,
to smoke cigarettes? How many years?

In how many countries
did you only know how to point
to your mouth and the words

for hello, cigarettes, and beer?
Where in London is the hotel room
from the photograph, you at eighteen,

shirtless, smoking before the open window?
Do you have a taste for pickled things?
How much wine do you consider

to be one glass? Tell us
about the coffeeshops of high school,
the lonely ones of college days.

Just the one grandfather?
And your father's heart?
Your mother's knees?

How long did you live across
from the substation?
The street constantly filled with taxis?

Even at night? How is it
that in your dream
your grandfather reaches

around your legs when you're standing
on the second floor, and he's waiting
by the open front door?

The Mountains of Madrid

She said her mom was dating Bob Dylan,
and if she were home, we'd have to steal
around the back. When barely a cherry
remained glowing beneath the ash,

she'd lay her head against me,
her hand making turns
on my stomach, and there might have been
an answer there

if I concentrated hard enough
on her breathing, the taste of her
a smoke blowing over me.
She said her mom knew Bob Dylan,

and I had grown up in a nowhere city
off of Highway 61, the son
who had the suspicion he was an impostor,
and our stolen cigarettes lit up

the faces of my friends like answers
constellating in the blank pool of night,
a mirror hung over the neighborhood park.
I reached my hands into the dark

and she said it wasn't her
I was looking for.
The stolen beers around the fire
of scrap lumber we built on the unpaved

road to the unfinished houses
held the answers in suspension,
and my friends and I went home,
desolate, for visions of brass beds.

She said her mom was with Bob Dylan,
and I stood out on the sidewalk
trying to work a door into the ice
with the dull edge of my boot's heel.

The Dance

What should have been the vision
          stretching before the curve?
What could I have done
          for insight? It's a tale
of dirt. Of things
          unplanned for rising
from the stone planter.
          I look in the mirror
and trace the scar—
          a fallen shepherd's crook,
a dropped question—
          and my finger
makes a double seeing,
          working along my skin.
What should the response have been?
          Where does the fear fall
if the pit is pure
          absence? I always suspected
intuition was the bowel's game.
          Feeling is a snake's
skin, not a cup.
          We danced in the living room
to Richie Havens's "Follow,"
          my eyes sloughing off

whatever self I had erected.

      It was more like holding you

inside a tightening circle

          while around us a circle moved.

Gold Coast

It's what carries things over, the interest
that brings us swept up into our futures,
like the surface of a bubble bulging into
the right now of things, where I place

my finger, push my face into the give,
always a surface ahead where I step
from the curb. Sure, in some meaningful
and not so meaningful ways, we're already

there, on that timeline where everything
has already happened, the Möbius strip
that never lets you meet yourself on your way
back around. Or imagine it as a movie,

a scene shot in a 19th century
banker's office, moments like fortunes sifted
from hand to hand before letting them fall
across the table. I don't know how to buy

my way back. At some point, the stream just split,
went sideways like so many chandeliers
of origins to light or drunkenly swing from.
Like the morning still awake in this city

when I could have stayed in her bed.
The cab ride away was too harshly lit.
And I have returned and have continued
to return, to be in love here. But yesterday,

when the pilot took an approach that led
first over the lake, there was a moment
when the water looked as if it wouldn't move,
never had, and forever compounded

beneath us, no current was pulling us back.

The Extra Welcomes You to Sunnydale

I had to be two minds, all day, all
        night repeating: You are dead.
You are dead, yet you live. I had
        to be one among many
who gathered for fights in alleyways,
        where lost families from any-

where suburban California came
        to be terrified. I
saw only maps and estuaries inside them. "Why?
        Because it's you or me."
And in the mirror, I pictured the kiss release
        twin flames at the neck, streams

I knew as desire, that called to my thirst—
        deep, atavistic, life
itself, the without-which-nothing fire
        igniting every part
only the sun—a greater fire—could burst
        to ash, empty this heart.

Expectancy

He places a pillow across my lap,
then lets loose a joke about saving dignity.
He wants to check my scar, and the whole team
descends from their orbit to watch his cold hand
test a red line the length of my stomach
that closes where the stomach had been.
From their fingernail's slice of cratered moon
they assemble the daily surgical theater
where I come and go, lifting and dropping my gown.
His fingers probe around the plate, reading auguries.
Then like a held breath retreating from stench,
the team deflates, the demonstration ended.
But today, there's special providence:
the pathology drops like a winged thing
wounded. Like the one I'd found on the patio,
its feet still curled around some absent branch.
The sparrow had the look of a toppled-over
sleepwalker. My hand stuck in protective layers
of thin plastic grocery bags, I was afraid
that what I touched would spark, would wake and fly,
even though that's what I should have wanted
for it. No readiness can cure that.

Lives of the Saints

It was a man rising through flames, or a man
                made of that fire who first entered
      my dreams, out from some crypt my child-brain

had placed on the hill leading down to our church,
         where I was prepared in the circles of tongues

speaking the language of fire to believe
            I was owed this, an afterimage burned
      into every dark room I would now wake in.

Doubt was never welcome at those sermons
        where hymns (dry and powdery cakes)

coughed up in our throats, while we were urged
           to concentrate on omega, the point
      in space my prayers—a breath always

beneath my breath—rose off to, for everyone
        left here, strung up above the pit and snakes,

and I wasn't supposed to have seen it,
           though for weeks after, all unknown faces
      appeared out of the house's cloaked corners

like the wretched and doomed forces
in *Raiders of the Lost Ark*, that cheap trick

of flesh melting like wax and milk poured
over mystery lunch meat that could scare
no one now. Something carries over, a broken off bit

knocking inside the disposal, some image you could identify
if only the scene would stop buffering. A belief

that you could pick out in a photograph all the space
between this fear and that boy watching the actor
crack his whip inside the air of the family room,

while out of earshot, his mother imagined
all the space between prayer and her saints

racked and flamed, pierced beneath the words
binding up the pages of her books, her hands
running out the thin chain of beads like the gears

stretching the cables that are stretching us over
the sorrow we were promised could get us there.

The Body Most Days

Suitcase of aches, aisle of discontinued
items. The assembly line proclaimed
to make things easier. Still, the product

proved fragile, inefficient, and difficult
to clean. Take this model here, or the one
before that—or would it be after?

What comes advertised as only gently used.
You're gifted what's at hand and submerge it,

draw it up, and submerge it again.
That motion repeated against something abrasive,

like a sound wooden board or your consciousness.
Just beyond the window, a crepe myrtle

with two white-winged doves, and three, now one
sparrow. You have to puncture the surface for air.
There will be no set intervals. You're swimming

in it all the time, even when you think you're not,
even when sleeping without a simple dream
in your fogged-up head. It's morning and somehow

there's toast and a window, your pain a single sparrow
jabbing seed from the grass. Even when you're asked

to play the role of villain, murderer, kidnapper
with a sudden change of heart—
Every theater comes equipped with lighted rows.

Portrait with Dust and Fingerprint

My one face, despite its many
disguises. Years of gold and rouge,
years of feathers.

The stocked-for-winter times, those
of the cheekbones' chipped mica.
You make it out from the photograph—

one poet young, one too young to be so old.
The year of lonely apartments
but good meals together. The knot

in the thread connected to this knot
here, which is the nature of thread,
no matter how tangled

or dropped with a plumb.
Years of cigarettes at box fans
wedged into windows

the first quiet minutes of morning.
The year fat then thin
with malignancy.

Because the face must be supported—
a pale post and leather coat,
heavy for winter, dark

as the shells scooped from around my eyes.
(You once wrote
the soul gets in like that.)

Whatever weather was happening
in that apartment is still,
by this thread, happening.

Even the other face that is dust,
as mine is now a smudged
fingerprint, greasy under the glass.

It was so easy back then
when all we had to do
was to walk out the door.

Cutman

—for S.P.

The training? The weight? I have this job and
it does me no good. There's the spit-back-out.
There's tomorrow's blackened eye and end-swell
smoothed along your puttied face to knuckle
the mousy blood from hiding. What odds now
have we been given there? Is your head still
intact, roped atop your shoulders' firm post?
In the notes you left, there's a regimen
of steps, of bobs and weaves, a diagram
for a microphone strung to the rafters.
The world mattered. The garishly lit ring
was only ever meant as an excuse
for the meeting of friends. The sport? Agon?
What draws us here feels like over-shiny
tracksuits. They've made this movie countless times—
hoodies and sweat, the frigid slabs of beef.
Just the other night I watched on TV
a young contender knock blood from a mouth
so strained, it looked to wear the mask of singing.

After X

—*"who dressed him in the earthy garments"*
—*Xenophanes, tr. Sherod Santos*

All becoming—and all that is—
    must come from earth, and where
earth has been, and where the waters
    came to separate it.

***

Even when young I knew there was a time
    for such questions—imagining
the car door torn from its hinges
    and my body a stone shot along

the tarred surface, or at night
    when the pull of sleep was a slipping out
into darker spaces, to be an object
    lost among other objects—

questions like: What is your name?

    Where are you from? How old

were you when the images brought back

    the scene outside the rocket's grainy eye?

        ***

And here, on this side, our feet touch

    earth where it would break off

toward sky, but beneath us the fall

    is a fall endlessly.

        ***

The architect made the garden

    for reflection, but with

the fountain stagnant, in need of repair,

    it's hard to sink into

transcendence. Still, the guard tells us

    it's okay to enter,

"to walk around there.

    People go inside and have feelings."

       ***

If the horse, the lion, the empty-eyed

      ox had the means and talent

for making, painting, and sculpture,

      the horse-god would be a horse,

      the lion-god a lion,

      the empty-eyed god

      slow like an ox.

       ***

"I saw him once," the citizen said,

        and when he closed his eyes,

    he saw himself.

"I saw her once too," the soldier said,

          and when she closed her eyes,

     she saw herself.

        ***

Credo: All that comes must come from

   earth; all that ends ends here—

let only dull gods speculate

   on the purpose of dust.

Vertigo

*—"The most painful state of being is remembering the future,
particularly one you can never have." —Søren Kierkegaard*

He said his mother thought it up, a bit
of spontaneous summer "edu-tainment,"
so his sister got the toilet paper roll,
and his mother held tightly to the end

while he carefully walked out the length
of the unspooling sheet down the sidewalk
for the whole neighborhood to see. "I'm at the start
of the universe," she shouted. The square

in his hand held the time of life on Earth;
his fingertips, people. Then they tried
a game of catch with the re-bundled mass
as a misshapen sphere. It was then the dream

started happening, he said, where he stood
at one end of an empty gymnasium, his mother
staring at him from the other side of the room,
and no matter how much he pleaded or yelled,

neither one would cross the bright wooden floor.
My father had told me about his recurring childhood
dream: a landscape, like a farm, with only a house,
a metal crane, and a tree, then an uneasy feeling

of watching all of this from very far above
while it sat right in front of him. When I was a kid,
I'd been more impressed with a tree so large
you could tunnel a road through it than I was

with Kim Novak marking a cross section of rings,
"Here I was born and there I died," my parents
a known but inscrutable presence in the room.
It didn't take too long to understand the tree

in the picture book they'd read to me, then left me
to read myself, was not really a tree, and the world
my parents moved in was a world carved to stumps.
But the story of Abraham was always a story,

and the knife and stacked-up altar were there
before the mountain and would be after. Once,
lost in the North Woods, my father drifted off
onto a soft shoulder that carried our car

sliding into a wall of birches. The next morning
I woke to find my broken arm had been no dream,
and no one was waiting in the hospital room.
I remember thinking: *it could be like this;*

no one will come for you. You must leave here,
barely a moment. In the movie, he tells her their name
means always green, ever living. She hates them,
each ring a future that takes no notice.

Nocturne with Emperor and Clown

I went out to greet the spirit, but it was an axe blade
    of light that sank its edge when the door closed
behind me, and it took a moment for my mind
    to adjust to the new dark, the total dark before things

regained their forms, but loosened, like paint knifed
    across a canvas at the point where the rocks end
and waves begin, where a wave falls within a wave,
    and Saturn's mouth dissolves his child's limb,

or like da Vinci's technique drawn from smoke,
    where he set curls around the Baptist's head, dropping
across shoulders and shadows unaccounted for,
    which is, after all, the tribute to smoke, a soft dark

exacted from the unseen, the hidden web felt
    across cheeks and lashes, evidence of the ghost
I had not come looking for, and I hadn't stood there
    for the short calls from the trees, not knowing

who made them, since I imagined the sparrows,
    jays, and white-winged doves off in their sleep,
or if it was the moon they called to, the blossom moon,
    or flower moon as they were naming it, friends tagging

and posting their own greetings an hour earlier
        on the coast, and I found it among the alien clouds,
requiems for clouds, barely the burst skins
        from which new ones had sprung forth, and I thought

not of the sparrows, or flowers, or the spider
        hidden in the lemon tree my fingers took up
the scent of, or the one withdrawn to the nasturtiums
        I could not smell but knew their flowers at my feet

were yellow, and cream pricked with the rust
        of blood, and orange, an orange like the moon,
the flower moon, but more solid and more delicate,
        and the moon was not an eye or a throat fully open

to sing something, or to drain the cut finger
        at the tongue, but a veil in the act of falling
against the earth, from whoever or whatever
        was sleeping, and faraway, and undisturbed by all this.

Notes

"The Only Spider Named by Charles Darwin"
Leucauge venusta, or orchard orb-weaver, was given its name directly
from Charles Darwin. *Leucauge* comes from the Greek for "with a bright
gleam," and *venusta* comes from the Latin for "elegant or beautiful." The
italicized lyric is Janice Joplin's.

"Then on the Shore of the Wide World"
The title is taken from John Keats's "When I Have Fears that I May Cease
To Be." The quoted phrase comes from C.K. Williams's "Tar."

"Course and Spiral"
The poem quotes Béla Tarr's *Sátántangó*; The Rolling Stones' "Salt of the
Earth;" Sherod Santos's translation of an anonymous Greek lyric, given the
title "Invitation to Oblivion;" and Seafood Health Facts.

"Cabin in the Woods"
The poem owes its title to Joss Whedon's film *The Cabin in the Woods*. It
makes references to the brutal killings of Trayvon Martin, Jonathan Ferrell,
and Corey Jones.

"How Much Tremor There Will Be"
The title comes from the "Dies Irae" section of the Requiem Mass.

"The Abridged Politics of Starlings"
Between 1890 and 1891, Eugene Schieffelin released one hundred
European starlings, now considered an invasive species, into Central Park,

which was part of his attempt to introduce to North America the birds that William Shakespeare mentioned in his plays.

"Forty Million Daggers"
The title is from Pavement's song "Two States."

"The Palace"
The italicized phrases come from the Palace Brothers' song "O Paul," which randomly came up on the radio in my car just after I learned I had cancer.

"When They Looked Up, They Saw No One"
Matthew 17:6-8: "When the disciples heard this, they fell facedown in terror. Then Jesus came over and touched them. 'Get up,' He said. 'Do not be afraid.' And when they looked up, they saw no one but Jesus."

"Nocturne with Emperor and Clown"
The poem owes a lot to John Keats's "Ode to a Nightingale."

Acknowledgments

Thank you to the following journals where poems from this book first appeared in these or other versions:

The Account, Bennington Review, Better Magazine, Copper Nickel, Delmarva Review, Kenyon Review, Love's Executive Order, New England Review, Oversound, RHINO Poetry, Scoundrel Time, Smartish Pace, Sugar and Rice Magazine, Waxwing, West Branch, and *Zócalo Public Square.*

The completion of this book would not have been possible without the immeasurable support I received from family and friends. My love and gratitude to Holly for being my partner, friend, and indefatigable foundation. Love and gratitude to my whole family for the time they spent with me, giving me the strength to finish these poems. Love and gratitude to Niki Clements, Michael Collier, Tim Crowley, Amber Dermont, Sarah Ellenzweig, Jennifer Grotz, Rosemary Hennessy, Lacy Johnson, Sally Keith, Joshua Mensch, Helena Michie, Tomás Q. Morín, John Mulligan, Patrick Phillips, Ian Schimmel, David Schlesinger, Kent Shaw, and C. Dale Young—your friendships carry me through. Love and gratitude to Martha Rhodes, Ryan Murphy, and everyone at Four Way Books for their generous work and continued support of my poems. I would also like to thank my colleagues and students at Rice University and Warren Wilson College MFA Program for Writers for their invaluable community and for giving me the gift of a life talking about the art I love so deeply.

Paul Otremba is the author of *The Currency* (Four Way Books, 2009) and *Pax Americana* (Four Way Books, 2015). He teaches at Rice University and in the Warren Wilson College MFA Program for Writers. He lives in Houston, TX.

Publication of this book was made possible by grants and donations. We are also grateful to those individuals who participated in our 2018 Build a Book Program. They are:

Anonymous (11), Vincent Bell, Jan Bender-Zanoni, Laurel Blossom, Adam Bohanon, Lee Briccetti, Jane Martha Brox, Carla & Steven Carlson, Andrea Cohen, Janet S. Crossen, Marjorie Deninger, Patrick Donnelly, Charles Douthat, Blas Falconer, Monica Ferrell, Joan Fishbein, Jennifer Franklin, Sarah Freligh, Helen Fremont & Donna Thagard, Robert Fuentes & Martha Webster, Ryan George, Panio Gianopoulos, Lauri Grossman, Julia Guez, Naomi Guttman & Jonathan Mead, Steven Haas, Bill & Cam Hardy, Lori Hauser, Ricardo Hernandez, Bill Holgate, Deming Holleran, Piotr Holysz, Nathaniel Hutner, Rebecca Kaiser Gibson, Voki Kalfayan, David Lee, Sandra Levine, Howard Levy, Owen Lewis, Jennifer Litt, Sara London & Dean Albarelli, David Long, Ralph & Mary Ann Lowen, Jacquelyn Malone, Fred Marchant, Louise Mathias, Catherine McArthur, Nathan McClain, Richard McCormick, Kamilah Aisha Moon, Beth Morris, Rebecca & Daniel Okrent, Jill Pearlman, Marcia & Chris Pelletiere, Maya Pindyck, Megan Pinto, Eileen Pollack, Barbara Preminger, Kevin Prufer, Martha Rhodes, Paula Rhodes, Linda Safyan, Peter & Jill Schireson, Jason Schneiderman, Roni & Richard Schotter, Jane Scovel, Andrew Seligsohn & Martina Anderson, Soraya Shalforoosh, Julie A. Sheehan, James Snyder & Krista Fragos, Alice St. Claire-Long, Megan Staffel, Dorothy Tapper Goldman, Marjorie & Lew Tesser, Boris Thomas, Connie Voisine, Calvin Wei, Bill Wenthe, Allison Benis White, Michelle Whittaker, Rachel Wolff, and Anton Yakovlev.